CLARK

88

COOLIDGE

SONNETS

Published in the United States by
Fence Books
Science Library 320
University at Albany
1400 Washington Avenue
Albany, NY 12222
www.fenceportal.org

Fence Books are distributed by University Press of New England
www.upne.com

Design by Brandon Downing
Printed in Canada

Library of Congress Cataloguing in Publication Data
Coolidge, Clark [1939-]
88 Sonnets / Clark Coolidge
Library of Congress Control Number: 2012951072

ISBN 13: 978-1-934200-61-2

FIRST EDITION

FENCE BOOKS are published in partnership with the
University at Albany and the New York State Writer's Institute,
and with help from the New York State Council on the Arts,
the National Endowment for the Arts, and the friends of Fence.

SCRATCH GLASS PARK

There's bound to be greenery in it somewhere
and white tacks   swarms on the bourbon
red at all points   nothing you could call a stop
white hunters don't keep very well   stick it?
where would us beings be without terminal consonants?
anyone here able to direct?   copy anyone?
this baby's going to stop up   clouds in the morning
hash on the barrelhead   we've heard too much in our youth
now it's sanitary but the boils are coming   we've had
the tip of the balloon a pen full of mud
ready to go?   I'll announce the hot mush
barricades in crossfire   unsufferably taut stuff meant
I could stand a bean or two   red or blue though
no whites   nothing to have to tether to

STOCKING DOWN

Tall spoken with a white brim head?
I got out of the habit behind the walls
sounds of plows   chickens   dynamite lighting
direct from Pitiful Wells Lusitania   why don't you
close your laundry hole?   patched in linoleum
I never had a chance   who's that?
brain soda victim with little on his ticker
what's this?   the Guns of Movietone?
long thin excuse for a pickle on a cake
Deuteronomy backing up at the Acid Palace
all you need is a Thing of Beauty maybe some joy?
the command to reload and a scissor moon
Cassiopeia down the stormdrain so intense
it won't matter who or what docks

RAG CHRYSANTHEMUMS

I didn't know whether to jerk off or kill somebody
I was so   learn to pull out before it's too late
cathedral ceilings in a polecat hutch on the level?
the dry bags roll   the words need a little salt
not much to touch up there doc   tubular
smells and well-plucked strolls   terrible thing
you never come in advance?   recall Enos Slaughter?
genius in a two-dollar haircut otherwise a madman
pushed by Dick Pictures takes a glug of dark colloquium
throat cut with a twelve-gauge   looks to me like
these people got cluttered to death   the police need
a motive and I got one!   deep purple in shades on
the lam with harhar toothbrush and ukelele
those Boise jerks had few dollars they should've worried more

A SPEECH DUMMY

Only angles have things   now which one
of you bums is Flaggy?   Vermilion Building
floor whatever version of the Non Dimenticar
Rita Hayworth just standing there back in the days
when we knew to use prepositions like wings
the Mahogany Building just sat there   it's a
boogie nest?   I learned about snow on things
the night the dummy's head came off for good
I couldn't say a thing   our hosts were in positions
the train pulled into the dock   the tea kettle hummed
there was a toad in the room   a condition to contact
blood on the surface of the moon that powder interior
for radio cubes and nothing cold under the sun
such an old console I didn't see the fun

A CASE OF OVERPARKING

She's got that raisin stare I'm looking
for a man with hands on his head
believe me will be back shopping for silences
gone loony on the mark a chaos near to beauty
expects to escape like mercy from the former owner
jet scars in the overhead certain ceilings
the true extent of the light poems? you got
something going? patterns on a wishproof wall
Lady Godiva in the driveway with the Dixie Cups
Kleenex residue Vivaldi on the radiator
Blue Marcus the last original you see
the jars full of eyefuls? drowning doorsteps
delicious buzzing hinge lots it's true
if a dumb enormous ash in extent

LIBRARY OF HAY

So slow death oft the onyx dolls
each in its own lab colors   rollicking encores
who's there?   do you want your museum
room infiltrated?   only the singing parts
terrible loss of air raid powder
entanglements poled on kapok
the last to be heard? this ploy of dolls
irradiated heads and curls of coffin wood
death is always plural here?   stolid
anyway someway still enters the frontway
through the water door to Manikin Lake
the throttles held down there you went to
hair school against my wisdom thus the
remnants spelled out there then coded there

SHINE

Cindy Hairpiece plays off the pages in her log
it's a nice set of virtues pianistically
somebody sending something out and not hedging
the prism remains weighted to the touch
I read the dispatch   hard ones given a nudge
my first gig was in Castor Alley untainted
untalented too so soon we brought ourselves home
a faucet on the corner of the house held me up
I can't explain   next is Cindy Partition
she leans over her charts and I see growth
wishing the same words wouldn't always come
in threes?   at all   teacher hits firewall
primates give up their habits far as anyone
the dullness of a magazine remains illumined

COMMIT TO WHAT?

Body rejects all over the blowback
I bet your moondust came in a can
a novel of no future   too late
became a beat memorizer   next day
thought he was Willie Stargel   blue ice cream?
lick it and you'll punt   have the stones of a monkey
broke one off and ate it well they were offering
the Rules of Temptation a local group
just try it you'll come up all drawstrung
life escaping from a pumproom I dunno
my tongue was just lying there
think I'll lie here and roll off
to sleep

WE DON'T CARE FOR AMERICANS

Not shit art at all but   stare at it
tentacles another huggy death   walk down
form corridors only to dream again   in L.A.
change of terms no limit   a chain wreck
five hundred pages later a summary and then
another   no intervening events   are those yours?
whatever an arena contains   hold onto your bulbs
so far from any sort of world right now
see them smoking over there? they're not friends
so can we see some art now?   a plate of grass
quarrels on the way to   you have maybe
a chewing gum waitress?   a tar mattress?
eccentricity circuited in place of what?
so he butts in where there's no art showing

NOTHING'S RIGHT ON THIS BALL

It's soup to the finish
you look like Jerry Lewis
taught to hunt for a living
back up   my treat
stop it will you?   the father
comes armed with clout
clothing a shabby shape   don't
be fooled by all this oxygen
we do have a container problem
if you run across any cement beware
raisins or drapes which is it?
the year ends on the thin end
you need Phil Spitalni lessons
that or the closest closet

THE DRAGON PATTERNS

Rides with the Dragon Vipers
water pockets elsewhere   no more private lives
soon will be gotten   a hustle about plain fields
diretissima nodules   starving frozen then
gone mad with road apples   wrong face in any mirror
the imagination's come about like a sloop but in ice
and wooden circumstances   my mother's stained wire fence
a stopping off perch   don't bother the fish cats!
the harm factor is plunge   they raise a dinner
called Yellowstone in Winter   hoo hoo hoo
my left shoe   took my answers off the air
this is an ode to Swollen Woolens   hear those cries?
stays cold in these hills   all the broken nighttimes
bargains of the hot belly deprived

PASSION

From the toaster to Teddy's crack
I'll appeal to the object right off fresh
the piano is nattering again   hey!
it's a lake autumn for fishing angels out by the falls
reflex a forced march faded folio version
ballet of the chaos   get up and apply to your apparel
as such to reflect and ride   buildings too small for
the journey   you'll do your dance in the coat I give you
these are the real figures   honks   skips honks
have lights we must have barriers   romance in the flies
shut it   you must ride in the light   take that!
coerce rehearse cohere!   I love you too well
the light inside is not penetrant   the kinks are slack
I'll come back as soon as the source returns

HANNA'S FACE

Hurry   these parking lots have too many doors
trips on her way up   takes to the trees
by the glass   hello press   hello minor
this is an order you must take   acrobat
even a tonsil flex and more come out
red dress of perfection senora Nobelle
a contrafood   I said give 'em junk   forth
we proceed from listening to listening and let them be
this is the margin cushion   we'll be by later
squeal and roar of tape   there'll be payment
and tears   send it all down the tube
I'll get around to   desk set to flat out absorb
music?   what do you think it has to do with?
here they come again those hurtling lights starting

REVOLVING GLANDS AND HUGE BLOND EYES

A rebate with every Glynis Johns album
for which there is no box   a mauve man in a white suit
limps along a river railing this will not do
these are lightbulb glass imitations of daylight
to us superiors those spheres make no odds   is this the
cabinet for Cargyle Heavy Liquids?   car leaves
tunnel like never   it's a sports girl barefoot in makeup
you see her wind her way without   she's winning though
been taking body lessons but come in   we feature
many varieties of darkness   depths of chest
in one   her car runs on divorce settlements
at which she toils like a sister   nice pointy little
paintings but there's no floor beneath this one
goodbye   why?   your name suits you like a suit

DROP YOUR ROBE

You wake up in a slip to a blank screen
then a bra with lips built-in it's all about architecture
good long talk with man looks like monster
you dig?   what's been done for you is uneven
so follow me in that bust-out dress found on you
hollow as you stand   answer if you can
The Lid of the World Is Off by Carmen Dragon
it's the pustule theme from not much of a scene
eyes on a tightrope the duration   here in
Anamorphic Forest of Arden you play
the beloved Soapy but don't trouble yourself
once a big girl of few lips you're confused
fussed with electric timelock in sobriquet gate
tubes of the stuff   shrapnel made of sapphire

TAPE BOY'S LOOSE

Came here took your Geritol and now it's all over
why you're sucking wet   I came tied
a thousand years to the date   sorry I can't
come before dinner   a ray glow intruding
beautiful outside are you being funny?
sat down a frump got up a liar   examine
your chest   is that also racing with the moon?
are there sexual scenes?   will I be made to feel
fudged?   card won't work?   guess that's what
you get for fueling with Bartok's Paprika
letting the barns out of the cows twisted one
now you will sleep on liquid benches just try
break that mirror with your pole dead center
make a good living interpreting peoples' rugs

I'LL GO LOOSE

Ghost of Flaps   nevertheless feeling fired up
must you lie so?   painless boy to no point
wrapped linoleum around the wandering mind
didn't I enjoy my girlfriend Doctor Symbol?
Mister Paff he wants to go over again
take that sibling off the rod   Mrs Beeping
wants to watch Twilight Wit and the Impatient Agent
a favorite among so many brilliant revolvers
cabochons to elaborate in the scatter space of
Cuckoo Palms   Elvis's glass under the giant conch
sound of the cracking coconut and off you get
up ahead it's all dragon butter and tape decks
there you'll be Launchboy master of the gas prongs
aper of all this world's shrinking progeny

A BUNNY FOR YOUR CUTS

Healing at the mushroom counter
he doesn't speak he just tweets
an insanity of misinterpreted surfaces
shoots out then lays back it's nutritional
an underbubbling that strives   edgy as
a volcano on its rims   stark tales of clay
mummery and subdivision you're getting close
the very word "tendency" sets a limit
the towel's your tightwad   a blowback magic
tunnel to Atrochia   use the furred muffs
Club Location opens its states and up-bucklings
lend me that mocha solder ring   the one
with the reciprocating bankruptcy cylinder
it's so good to finally be all throat

CHAOS IN THE WEST

Care for a spot of blood?
the specimen was   petted
that pause was delicious   frontal though
it had to   I don't now know
what I'm looking at looks like
well as nothing does   ask Bill Tragacanth
Tyro Loopy   better send in the preenforcements
nobody's that great   so you took out monk insurance
a bargain but no knockout   check the old tunnels
watch the haberdashers   treat your mom to a lull
I played one once in a throwback
thanks to complications of the Nutter Theater
The Bunk of Terrace Mound   with the milk bar
it was all left turns from there

PULLEYS AND OUTTAKES

Soil drum timbales a shoeshine can
in halibut car   the four-in-hand your favorite
hospital corners not so much   a motorhead
block the principle of the thing   an adjustment
most devoutly to be sought   hear the mechanism?
we took it all out in a paper bag like a plaything
I never did form the words so well   how about
a list of every one you ever used?   you have
a free hand and before you know it three days have passed
or so it's thought   I have a philosophy problem
how many more bodies do you think it will take?
that muffinlike substance found on the Moon
won't go away   you'll see it glow on demand
icicles will form on the smallest member

TOLD SO HE KNEW

But luckily in his case the octopus was incompetent
jam hours later   a paradise of sinkers
he was the Rake of the Wed Rich is it not?
sorrier men have surely been born can't you tell?
the octopus waits at the bottom still incredible no?
is she pissed?   this octopus was called No Names Please!
otherwise there'll be a letdown   anyway it comes up
bastidload by bastidload   blow the octopus
a puddle slowly forming beneath   best organs in the capital
started with that sucking sound but guess what? no hole
that night he dreamed Tim Roth told him that
film editing was a commie plot   some nightmare
not the door but what comes through it that's framing
declared on the floor of the world's largest aquarium

AN UNCOVERY

To know death you have to fuck life
in the gall bladder but how can it not
know what it is?   backs into these situations
barely and widely   a sampling of semens
the sewing of   blue waters for human brains
who'd have thought?   you must precipitate the nectars
so there's force in these bloods   variorum
edibles   you may play the Wagner now   full bore
the fluids out of anyone   these smell coils
they lay draped in the foyer a remnant of
the marbleized flesh   add a motor on
the cycles in ambient chains   a ropy dildo also
ein zwei mental guy   watch the eyes
you will see a woman assembling and no bumbling

ARCANE HEMISPHERES

Something is wrong with the literature of this blood
maybe a tool baron?   help must be brought
to light this legend   take the taxis away
clear the blocks   I will have all flesh riven
gestural lengths of shadow and echo bulk
the Armbruster is the name of the monster this time
but I don't anymore take it that   anything!
the vestibules beyond the outer rooms will tell the tale
Uncle Cecropio you may dust my broom
palest crystal master   what is dead must remain
beyond the alternate fleshlike regions   let it go
Artoo will find us out   heard a cry in the mirror
located in the funnies but so graceless in class
the whole night shines a brass hole in my tongue

FRESH MONSTER

Sometimes the news business descends to
long dark corridors made of cinder block
even its very source primitive all the way
Pickfords it was said but maybe not   got a Coke?
better not judge the guitar you find wanting
pretty much nothing but apple fiber and horse tonsils
but that's garbage   it's not?   sure as you're shirtless
oh good a movie where you can't see anything
consult the Book of Sewers by Colonel Sanders
Doctor Waters?   he's gone away Mrs Torrance
got a running scene?   call Mister Bongo (Jack
Costanzo)   is this the body of the text?
it's off the charts but who's the duller now?
the body's gone and these footprints are our own

TENSION AT TOMATO POINT

Soon will be crystal clean I don't mind
the copra supply farmed off to outerwhere
this time prism light has a grey grain to it
Chisel Day   the tour maps are clogged
Flowers For Superman I never read it
may have to drive the terminal herd
plucked from hoister beds and coats
level deep if hermeneutic   catch a
later analysis or bus leaving there from
my toys ate me   not to mention the Mylanta
cork bred in sulfur subsidy tanned by the Moon
brained by the poem   so stick it right there
they found tears on the platform   ants in hives
blast and you never know where they'll land

A CRYSTAL SAW

Separate these rocks and they pop like bulbs
a gruesomeness unforeseen   sloshed unconsciousness
do I smell the smoke plume of a pearl?
consider   substance tootie sort of thoughtless durable
comes in two suns   at least one a new one on me
cribbed from the oversoul?   only the housing missing
pauses then strips to the bunk without oxygen
net force one lap   I heard the shot
whole hillsides stretched in two   dial the brass code
these things hatch into worser others
the doorframe leaks   the pages are damp
somebody must've taken a piano to that one
but how far can one hike?   we got no radio
well you need to be brighter   live by the lamp

PUTTERS

Go pep   you're slack   she's got
the small tooth touch   no finer brains?
time to call up toast   sharp jelly rock drill
sack of this brand new metal rains
down from doorways   cast brads   retreds
honks must've come from the Moon so dull
takes taste test goes overboard finishing
call the boulder squad they'll have nippers
toggle screens with blunt displays   no heat
but braided retro   got a map protector?
this is the age of simple hammer-produced cell division
somebody named Buttrey invented the presentation
be better off with bladed substitutes
peelings from the left side of the road

THE PRICE OF SO MUCH

He's in a state of pitch fuck
diurnal?   secondary smoke Palooka
relax   have a Creosote   there's guys
with aluminum tear ducts up there   solid
I have caught the concrete and it does resound
well it's time we heard from somebody   and
these are the Streets of Shenanigan an endless
recording of closing doors has an air of finality
the andirons of cars?   as Yellowstone goes
so goes the nation   dipstick licorice and everything
not as if we all should get a free ride
those plates are soon empty   of rutabagas too
the wishing well is now a lap pool   last seen
warming hands on Mickey's Caldera

CORNHOLIO IN A VALE OF FLOWERS

You'll have sizzling finds if
brash plaques due in September just as
the club meets for the last soda a stumbling factor
standing there face full of false lake
fused in the walls   you'll feel better
there's lamp black and then there's magic block
a trombone insists on coming in here   listen
breakfast food!   get sewed up you don't shut
the tiger burns what?   the evidence dumbass
you could feel the crusts left and a little bridgework
or bookmark?   why is the dyemaker wearing
a rebel head?   going along motorized
leaves you whistleless no snappy comebacks
tracking damaged   the birds remain to be rounded up

THE SKIN HAD TURNED

I remember those lamp paper rooms with the
hoist vise patterns   someone grasping out
till it's all gone   what's been done?
the skull block dropped a full inch is what
bay rum pushed to the back of the cabinet
built-in wood painted white with silver clasp
stood on tiptoe high above the first floor
through a crack   a split for bones and finds
the Clouter Society as younglings yet to be lost
behind the gauze was it a smile or a wound?
crossed out crossed up crossed instead
tipped with blunted pencil see verso
tells the tale   certified Ma & Pa Greenish
beasties beneath a covered metal hole

VOLCANO HOUSE

A patty really was that the gist of us?
the mottled seal of what's drawn tight
lifted at midnight?   a melted message
loopy plot at best and so's your other
stand up and salute the trace   a bluish glow
you'll only humiliate   subside   go by
gone world colored in at a slant   a realist
puzzle with tunnel sort of porte-cochere
paisley tied in the midden and great billboards
of blemishes blown up to stride the land
no more Burma Shave to be saddled with
nostrums mainly phantoms of a covered spot
flowered lid   you walk in one door and out
drift peg   the crater now smoking a little

CAN OF PUZZLE WICKS

The bright bat lit a Saigon byway
never to be found to be an outlived penny
blossom token the first forest you come to
the novice has dibs   that internal movement
the head placed in the lap just as choice
mishandled it so the joining wall snapped
a trick of the watch the house does not open
you can only write in a southerly direction
how's that for a grace note or two bars
for nothing?   deep pile browns trip in abeyance
a slot in your life the parallels are scary
tongs silicified in onyx bulk rank truck
no one anymore needs we grew such depths
the tonal motors could raise your pique

BROOD OF A HEARTY SKULL

Comes the time to table that lamp
a reading map will no further blacken
could singe you in circles type faces
the crystalline stubs once left it did
we matched as we watched
the tuba unlock   the trellis choke
a radiolarian loose in the garden
down at the dark end where lights are slim
pond weights of whatever fancies you
remove to cut and paste   line your lids
the crops resist the broom in need
the pump broke down the water to a starch
complexion was all that day's rage
coat and sprocket   an eye's removal

A STAGE VERSION

Cut my thumb on your cut thumb
effendi at the end of the day
I pursed my blood a slice of the deft
ness damn you and your shed principles
tear the mica off one hank of the sky
reach Placebo's Rest then reset tank
tank tonk   those elaborate levels of hover
cops raise duels for end up amounted to
ever raise duels for the end up amounted to
ever after nuts about meaning combines
restart those beds   Shawangunks
trilobites trembling you'll see extending
the stars like pills mounting up   it's frank
this crust of repetitions that tell you
a thing   and no more telling hocus pocus

A LEATHER PENDANT

Many odd entrances including the piece of cake
you get up behind them through the river
cracking to set it and whip up stew edges
the icing's on the grunt   we have intent
feel short?   never give in without a shirt
the man had polished his level input
these stories without bulk pinned in tight
once nailed to a stop   another of the sort
there's a plenty   so's to have it figured
lined in red lead the exhaust vent on the Sphinx
pouring with originals   luster of vugs
entrenchment entails reversed refills
the primer is salt in a feldspar labyrinth
you sure?   as the velvet starts to show

SUR LE ROUTE

Orotund for certain
the pliability file is quicksand
hope to tin a song melt
mean to air out the taps
here's Man Who Shatters Thing
but the substance is grey down and out
some day have to stop   save on notions
the motors ran out of tobacco
so be sure to   how slabby dealt
the decor increased itself   bring shovel
ladder and peppermint dipstick you know
drama bolt set on morning tension
this writing implement has run its course
may have to move my house

FORSAKEN PEN I'LL FORGET

Reality be dashed   I live in the quick
no bulk   sat there   funny   things happen
those dark swimming ways   architecture
hospitality   a flesh wound   the Duke of Earl
the real what's left when you don't sleep
even if you do or especially   no prizes
those dispatches   flakes off an iron bell
left on the avenue with the kliegs   unsung
the tiny human esophagus what a conundrum
where memory is a lot of dead hair   as a child
I held it to the light   the world there
in those common toys   breathing on the weights
measuring spoonfuls   nothing to say
wide as the rest of the empty way

WHERE'S MY HONEY?

A thermal city plumb
center of Magic Middle
I saw the flash   there's a hole
in the Volcano's fur apron only visible at night
and even then   Telsa had a hold on the world
just a brief time   he heated everything
usually his first move   a result still with us
Doctor Day is here   coils of dope   gathers of wither
received a tiny postcard of a playing card
held all the royal secrets in those pastilles
get right down on the floor of the machine to see for yourself
and who did I find sitting in my chambers?   Lord
Coldmouth   Allardyce to you ducks
I live in the place of infinite cats and hats

STARTS FROM

These people they just throw things
bread loaves even malt tablets
mysteries of every stripe
the very idea   how it all carries on
nougat or cat's-eye   obligation or terror
hear how the roofs still shake
even the lantern used as a horn
the mountain as shade
its crystals are growing dear
I could show you on the map
how music changes in the sun   the moon
a draft   the whole frontal catalog
some sense to the world in these
not want to stay but never leave

SYMPATHY FOR RADON

First off takes his measure of pins within
next to the telly our cow watches through the window
took off bra but the blouse didn't go
saucers came instead they rule around here
wedding postponed but the landing is on
pen points of alarm light on the mechanical frog
they could start warming things up from there
starring Paul Hemostat and Nan AimOfItAll
no production design only the names
American History Ladder Company Ten only a few
could attend   meet the creatures!   listen up but
they won't call back   piano down an empty corridor
trail of the hollow dog in the days before furniture
they left all the doors unlocked   people were a bore

SEEMS TO ME NO LESS

Then my television stopped on me
a nightmare of weight loss and doorbell tension
committed to the dialogues of Airborn Pall
removed his eyes along with the rest of his face
I'll just leave them on the table sir
such an awkward waffler from Mudkirk
the Radcliffe of his time and territory   a fly
lit and kept on lighting till I crossed my eyes
a flood of ideas on a boardroom wall
along with the time it took you   huh!
this doorlock is a revolver telephone!   how's
the list of everything you have left to do going?
here in Baresford Woods there are no doors
though what would make you think?

YO DOORLOAD!

Couple days and we'll have you all sewn up
you should have brought a doll of that dog
in the first place this town doesn't have time
they never voted for that treatment hey Crawdad
I'll wait over here   you'll wait where I say
you'll wait please an anchor steak I'll have
people in farm duds get up and walk out
into the silence of silliness a conundrum
all the glass in town blows out at once
better climb on in and toot   don't miss the takeoff
my radio is ruined and so's the car it came in
plus my can of dreams   tell me what happened?
the fog horn sounds and we're back in New York
where the jig is always up but nobody subsides

AFFECTIONLAND REPOSITED

Care to take a pee on me?   I'll have that
drink now   things in the wrong order   Blue Moons
dusty sacks and fronts on the right   want to go
away for a long yawn?   puts an end to that
like lava blocks a road to the sea   something
we learn to talk about like The Appointment of
Lost Chests misplaced in a swale they said
it's getting hard to   he loves how bouncy they get
hard to stop once you've donned silk ask Nancy Allen
from here on the plot begs sense   they get in
a cab for the sake of God or a bake sale?
now who is this?!?   the cast members evidently
have yet to meet   watch it they'll melt green
stuff comes out   your trip is definitely off

THE NORMAL ARE STAGGERING

Paul's surprised there's a carpet to be called upon
thinks he saw something   else it was an odd head
strung by the highway comes to the table on his knees
want to look at some drawings?   no and no
why don't you come with me?   no rational choice
I'll have the Marines show you out
you'll get this marble glow sheer to the floor
a make-believe hamper full of surprises
that's a powerful pencil sharpener you have
felt in the gut or is it the red dress of poetry?
you can't win prizes with an agate sponge
you can?   desperate to buy one a drink
Paul has eyes   owns a vaporizer but doesn't
house strangers as Wally Shawn as The Earl proposes

NOW RUNNING IN BLUE BACKYARDS

The brain makes less and less sense
as we proceed with this sum of all miscalculations
private hair on tap   hours to spend on substance
got a postcard from Jesus   Guy Jesus and he
wants it back   the wrong side of those trees they
just keep giving with the heat blinks they're cool
like no one anymore is   now what do you think you are
gubernatorial?   that's a thought high on eggs
I'm the Long Mailman but I'm on vacation
my wife's in training she went to sleep and woke insane
there was this highspeed sound inside a church
I walked to it   been working on it for years
smelling of gastropods and suction and it gave me a notion
tiny people having a meeting making a glow

WORST NEWS POSSIBLE

Haven't got a feel for much anymore not even
tugs at my straps   lumps in the substance
Marge Underhand there tagged my shorts
witless but fundamental we were
grilled by the Great Dead in their time
the show everybody called The Widest Licks in Town
let's talk   they found a horizontal hexagon
right here in Butter City behind the stationer's
we went all blubbery   care for a summary?
the braille's gone cold   give me five
you no longer appeal   the monster's gone grey
summers from their tins?   there are suggestions
caterpillars gone to seed   an Acropolis dust
this bus emerged from behind Sacramento

A FELT SUCCESS

Learn how to put things will you?   the pencil
won't stop probing   miracles occur down the tube
ink in your shoes through a flatter hat you couldn't
run   a whole airplane lost in the Atlantic
never to be done again the Pacific gleaming
put on orange pants for trawler duty
there's something in the learning glass apparently
peppermint will improve you Palmer Method
she's alive but she's a mess   torque you see
that's an idea   an alum shield the duration
THUD   somebody's here   the pain will kill her
the blood will hurt a lot very much can't stand it
the survivors stood on a shutter while the sun
made with the steady blinks and moved multitudes

BENT ENOUGH FOR YOU?

But do you understand what I'm not saying?
blow the anesthesia   top drawer   linked soups
hydraclaws the magenta of a styptic smile
blinks there's some loss   people there of no concern
triceps beyond belief   pyrites in a tin dish
danger in prose   stumbles on a stair
thread roots on Altair   I'll bus you to the cosmos
things you don't want here   the forest leaves
police abandon station   the flag goes down
where are the clowns in this town?   turgid?
bunk   they give even the pope a tryout
my job is to explain them   Pelee shouting
cigarettes on springs as the landscapes accumulate
we'll have to bargain for a few faint fogs

ONYX CAPSTAN USELESS

I've got a snore in my nose even a shovel wouldn't
what's in that bag?   only those who have to
a diurnal calcite substance empty enough if
I had a hunch it'd be a smidgen
got no more misty opportunities
the monster had iron ankles and no peace
they tried to build a missile base on his rock
you could smell the blob on the wind take me
there?   that cow's a fan of Eno's
must've spent the night   a stone the carving block
bites   hey!   there's no penetration not even
a shoulder strap   you cop to it?
I called it the mystery snap but it came out
nobody survived the Battle of the Shove

TESTING THE MONSTER

Is the drought ready?   I thought they
brought it to a head   the monster thinks
it's time   calls Doctor Artaud   there's
a forest of thermometers   the nightmare array
they're apologetic but warm water is always local
amber turns lethal   ants are released
Dadgum Vitamins useless and what's to come?
even the universe is lunch for something   if you knew
the end you'd be more than bored   they'd
lop off your shoes   the pipes the pipes
are impossible Danny   makes haste to pluck
the Magic Twanger Mr Bradley Mr Martin you know
Artaud's name is mud but these are particulars
the rest are as interesting as dental proposals

THE MONSTER FOR GRANTED

Ask for Vlad I mean   the tust came
out of the museum everybody happy stop time
filter back unleavened opportunity for husk products
line two a hash of the missing transits
the shit has hit the front   gales for miles
bar tap deep   Girl With the Pinchbottle Bra
a crisis of ground glass proportions in pencil musk
as you see it is perfect hands-on voltages
fluid appendages on forced birth treadles
I'll take a lodging in North Beach times past
run it out largo to fragments of sentiment
we'll be horrible to others but same to our own
an overarching oblivion patched if pensive
the world's just this racket

YOU'D NEED A SEPARATE SUN
TO RUN THIS MACHINE

Groaners we called them just off the coast
stern little baby bean drops fought for and
prayed to   a slice of right as rain
we are The Terrible People popeyed and rumpled
comatose or rugose it makes no odds
I'm a doctor   have a tryout   we call these
Hampton Tongs   postures on my mind
walks off in perpetuity   a foggy papoose
munching on minerals found by the side
tuberoses and beryl barrels indisputable terms
a cure for gravity?   here is Doctor Seize
a tried ingenue used to soot on the rails
the big surprise a nostril like a trench
not to mind the smell and still traveling

TOO MUCH WORK

Submission to a submachine waddling
books a matter of paper padding
needn't burn yourselves off in despair
see the discs?   that is the correct spelling
not to bother to dig deeper here is the pen
the inevitable pollution of pictures
taped to the mast   nose and throat
specialists will just thrill so prompt
you're waiting on what?   a new jockstrap?
the melody is from China   like DingDongs?
crystals in the harvest nest they swing and sway
you could see the starling plain   uprooters visible
atomic numbers clicking in this capsule to nowhere
I'll sign you sing   the pool is cement

BLUE SODA RIGHTS

Step in here but don't trip on the light
your offspring well he's narcotic
the spansules include his birthright
a planet with practical belts
life tenders?   op cit swaybacks
sweet as we all were told to back to
a toy magnet if there was such a boyhood
a personage made up as a harp
the grey bone protruding   a talking snake?
jelly squid?   the rustle of reparations
a possible autobiography in flocks of
favorite spoon handles all on the march
we'll end up having something I know it
the topspin in its own plane a swirl of terms

STAYED

Solid   I didn't know you baked
collected the lids   snored till rip tide
snowing it was   all out of oxygen
a sort of gas fit liberal as a tree
you're a snort victim   Downunder awaits
grown as paper as a book we used
pepper as a damper in the cloning of times
the clanging of brute substance a boutique
there's no stopping   a cribbage to link things to
bobbing wallets and wobble strings   ostriches
striking matches on endless card and stuff such
that the neck blows its chances at any upright flair
noting all the built-in mustn'ts herein laid
no system to these days

AN ORGONE HEAP

This father is a little too   prong
this may be the Abode of the Snow Apes
a cabinet full of calfskin drumheads
you drink like an Apache and the fuss over
pass that blasted tray comes true   come away
you like to open little steel boxes?   *ocupado*
hey mom   you playing with the bay rum again?
the A-bomb went off as you watched no eyes
but still it grew at the bottom of the pool
began to strum at the barricades in a stretto
more's the pretense   what if the water crystallized?
what if they had a copy made?   so what if
you chose to be a barrel slave?   that
was at camp and we couldn't stop floating away

BOWLING FOR AGATES

The broughten refuse to its room
made dizzy we all made our wakes
abysmal in length the rest string films
one ignores though they do move even take place
The Favorite Flames singing at the edges
cloak pot tumbles inchoate attracted
the clock is a magnet to all it surveys
an avenue is open to these gadgets of light
quirks or quibbles in an overall heightening
stuck to the rude or increasing go-forth
clips it's true you get to go over
get gold-carded every entry watch her curtsy
this summertime the living is a pocket of
a cubism of the strictly cutting

SOLIDITY

O great gleaming golden green at naptime
such that the crimes of us battlers
extend the velveteen balloon narrow as breath
take seat or tree   the values of this lumpy lawn
a landscape whose whistle ran down as all
those animals on the run or hunt we'll see
fish come true in alleys locally puddle or no
we felt like a sort of guest sauce around there
pumpkins made of gelatin width of a screw
plastic modeled novelties and knickknack ropes
sandwiched looseleaf where the offspring molt
keep their truck   cork thoughts
a pity that trench so long in filling
the thing came out of the night in training

TRUST ME TO CROSS YOU

A complete docusaurus the only one in the industry
a docklike flap attached post-formation
a duck shoot in the name of progress shirtless
when the games come you'll be a shoe-in
reformation solution at long ebb a fuel cell
make the call   mastication of an upchuck
alteration by degritude worn in the flesh
an obstacle tube Mr. Boilant scrubbed poppity
glub off the Gaspe Pendule jargonfree
the world a massive blot or gum wad
these people are monkeys with the hair shaved
based on little in this whirl to stand up to
ready for a ringtail argument ancillary experiment
it's a form of excitement   a rule hole

EASY

Probably another Helsinki for Moscow
not very well directed   just a hole in the zone
but I didn't want to say   it doesn't pay to do
your field work   kill them   skip the dough
prop your shoes in a train window
the plot contorts and you turn a blue hand
the laundry runs out   the brain was late
you'll have to walk into this wooden church
better bring your clamps   read Costigan's Needle
tired out commencing souls as backup the layabouts
prewar retred jobs come here to a hill of beans
a Mayan highwayman who just fits the cooze
the Rifleman and the Whore take off or leave
some things even a crystallographer craves

READ ONCE

Put on this wig and fiddle with those bottles
weak hands in a vast landscape   resultant
the effect of certain chests   see if you can
set this safe   a potpourri of betters
there are certain Houdinis   obstacles here
the pen flows where the brain cramps
the city blows only the museum remains
a laying-on of wee surprises   use no orioles
there are other-colored collars   statistical fillings
moldings of the Gold Octet   those boys
occupational blizzards at cop-out speed   were you
a Nazarene?   a localizer   bittersweet   fat port
the fog is a washout   come home
no matter the obstacle falls   come

LOP

Who is this one?   dotes on radio sodas
or one airplane soda   turns out offspring in
bed sheet hesitancy   these people thrive on
sow bugs and their expectorant dusts
not to come near them   there's a crisis of humps
illuminated by or with what?   a video blur
laid aside quarts and quarts of Eastern Europe
that ice-bruised light   a leitmotif beyond coast
that room is gone   a work in baskets or barrels
heard the one about the junkie and the monkey?
forgot his keys and shook the fat out
this in the days of experimental belts
fleece balls and Whitman Samplers precasted
you'll walk over rooftops as no one

FRANCONIA AS PLANNED

There is nothing but a bubble here
mostly   a crust of rainbows   lake shoes
you'll fit   the bulk of the series will wait
Champlain and its toasters   fiddle fish
the search is on   I am the Tracer
broad form of face and toil spectacular
ocular with missing moons out of minds last night
corked off into a stall   the Grand Mucilage
tooting will signal its arrival   top spelunker
untraceable gone tinkering no lugging allowed
those later silences tempered up the rat pole
lives to be stripped   takes to be sold   solid
of course not   that's the whole point   a black
market in Love Square long as you don't sleep

STARTING EXPENSES

I was visiting tobacco   only
I couldn't seem to   not a mention now
there is no justice in dessert   let's pretend
the vision clicked anyway   drew away from defeat
so long   that cat not allowed another mistake
but that was back in the Palmer Method days
would you like some light cheese?   pretense
you have yet another in that yellow box?
dear boil   you gotta be kiddin' me!
life's grand folly an occupational hysteria
first thing?   Monkey Beach no phones
I was this kid and R.I. loomed
large in my disturbance   no holes in
the nighttime but I was learning the lights

FAST ENOUGH?

Okay Deucy   my handwriting it's not
then the sun rings down   marshlight
a tubelight   the rings of Jupiter not
to dramatize your traumaturgy   those extras
pictures of Picasso at the starting line
don't groan   Billy Bartell over there
existence must've been out that day
you're puffy   thanks Max   same back atcha
a sink full of ruined drinks   moist sconces
emptied corridors that no more lead
a bellhop's idea of bread than a doorstop
doom   plain as a clapper or dipper in matrix
you'll have to return for the rest of your life
I left my helmet   forgot my license

DOWN AT GRANNY'S CAVE

Anyone interested in art is welcome to shoot up the place
auto mechanics washing down church sides
an iron clock interrupts the grammar lesson
thumbtacks in the coffee you better listen
a split second blink could do it   kill some
too few downturns in your m's   pouting over
a box loading operation   some temper with your tunes?
reflections in the snow?   nobody'll ever
you mean it?   lot of stone too much telephone
yellowjackets as a coat   nightmare as a lock
then only a peck of lemons   nobody cares where you are
the eve of optics   Orlando Cepeda knows
The Shadow stirs   losses all around
the creek turns into a reservoir and explodes

THE MISSION

Mars that wobbly rock
on Mars they caught this groundslide
alright?   let's see those tits
once a body of thought   now?
just more silliness   (squawk!)   your point
is?   dig Mars   home for the homeosexual
so where did you learn to drink?
care to propagate?   and on that note the stars
come to a conclusion   no more humanities
Gyro Gearloose has a query   are those
beer drums down there?   are we stopping?
now that every front is locked   located
endured   activate primary dudes
no more floorboards

DON'T MOVE

Is this the Marisol surface?   there will be
no teeth   wood lot dreams
a zero gravity fire   look at will
you won't design your own capacity
one day algebra could come thudding down
what's that you're hiding? your semen collection?
the last dried-out traces of the humanities
and you're done   the glorious arrival of something
at least something lit up ahead you boys
you must clothe yourselves in GoTex
a green can explodes inside your thoughts
hemotoad reaction pretty close to life eh?
to propose a hill right here for spite?
for accumulation and the subsequent launchings

THINK THIS

You don't understand   from now on
we'll have grey fun   lodged in the skull
it seemed a mind or violin frog?
real striper teacher   a car cheat
the clearance to admire sheer doors
the rest suspended by naked strands
couldn't make up their minds   was it
a home or a gallery they lived in?
a most tiring mist had come over them
so they attended bed   turned off all that stuff
had been speaking the wrong language all their lives
please sharpen those   the basement is full of Serbs
I'm positive   as wrong as I've been
the field is full of notes not dates

ON JUKE FARM

Cracked up so
required care
we had seen them fumbling in their clothes
cost one hitch   even seen anyone blanch?
he's got a hot head   it's a cold hand
give me time somebody   curl the walls
I choose the one with two stomachs
even the music in a bad kiss   you just have
to stop sleeping   it's over   try chest cover
you're telling me the Buddha lived in a cloud chamber?
I'll tell you   nothing but breathing   I'm occupied
hello   you qualify for the Life Lodge
no great shakes but you should expect
a life-size photo of Goofy in extremis

ON THE ISLE OF BORAX

This bed was made from silk rods
feels like   ready for the postmortem?
novels go under the shower before they're
ready to read   records go under the stars
prepare to stare things clean   this all started with
meat and logs   are you sure those are the nipples?
turns a corner and shakes her tail   this was on
the way to Powell's whole block of books
doing fine thank you all   have we been friends?
back when we lived on the top floor of all
but who are these people?   the color
ample followed by dropped cymbals and falling lightbulbs
we crowded together and then it was over
a thing wearily so eerily caught   just

THE VERY LONG PIECES

Just before the lights went he signed a blank
check with feces upsetting the populace
why they untied their shoes   called themselves Joes
aimed a penis with their ties   one more jerk
and we're done   an audience filled with substance
you could witness it fine from just two cars over
quite enough glass thanks   all
the lighthouses went broke at once it was noticed
but not for quite a while   they had been out of
date for years and that date had come due
abode chosen for its alley   source of BB toys
now presenting Suzie Brillo   you'll miss her
the stuffed animals all scratch at that
to lead the tempo with brickbats

SOBER IF NOT SOMBER

I happened to be thinking but then and then
the biography would revolve around living flesh
firelight and powder keg massages   let's go
even those attitudes borrowed from Cancel Farm
directors of cement mixers and dope salad
the women were crazy there they opened
for anybody   even Monkey Stern
Nancy Billfold   Attorney Bark Weld Esq.
handled candy bearings with mighty calm fingers
portage after low-slung portage no fakes
were you upset at the obscenity?   believe it
I was carded at my age (29)   everything spun
out of the water walked the rest
turned haze

INSTANT PROPERTY

The laughter gets too loud I climb the rooftop
book by Pinter   Tommy Pinter
nobody take hostages now just try flambeau
join the Idol Tossers Union it's free
moves by Hallstrom   nerves by Boston
last chance for the Secrets of Tacking Revealed
the meat gets together now   we'll confirm
the body runs out of paint   no problem
short stringers I guess   when I paint
the wall snaps back and we tune out the showing
when we left our next to last fancies we left
for Boulder and a high old time   a totality
more mercurial we shouldered like stoves
the women all leaned out from their curves

A SCREAM IN A BOX

There's a miller in your hair you moved nextdoor
there's no taste like bona fide mouthwash
turn of the car at the end of the road
steady up Powder Boy the clots are about to descend
a fairy dockhand was napping could've been a lot worse
only takes two minutes   let's pretend   you couldn't be
carefuller but they're moving   a funny time to
be moving   I've collected all my shadows
no prob   bum steer   quik-pik lunch ideas
flounders   pets that carp   waits on the door to burst
let's set up   or not?   there's a sewer just under
the paperweight   there are even warming signs
Mae Wests   always quite a bundle of that
there are other uses for fat

AND MONO DOGS

My billfold sprung a tab   short a bit
I'll be   the numbers stuck to the trunk wished
I had knowledge of villages then did so
flashes from all sockets a nice day
top browns everything now on a scraping sound
over by the power towers   once bitten I walked
lo-fi canapes and worn rarebit siphon off
there goes the old tan beast give me some stuff
I'll call Washington if you don't Ma Cellotex
more stinking toast?   your keys Mister Keats?
it's just these bulk goodbyes   logarithms
afraid our bellies won't fit these chairs
blow it out the vacuum microscope
don't wait until everything's shut

CAUGHT ON THE NETWORK

These kids have baseball eyes
drawn on a bedsheet the face explodes
Superman dies   we'll have to endure
I'll have to look   it up   no more truck
hillarity's attached to a wheel   slim control
an orgone booth I bid on on a whim   ultra
go-getter also a lamplighter though not so old
are you the dead honcho?   Novocain shipment
back of the closet along with the eternal wastes
bellicose gumption and we have the photographs
dope by Arp toast by Ernst but only in snatches
welcome to the Urbane Mine   parrots fading
fit for the oxidation hole   pencils to peanuts
diamonds among the lab samples everybody's nose opens up

COME GONE

He looks over his own eyeline
have you ever meant to be a joke?
played a game called Infectious Faces?
are you sexual in nature?   but this was all
meant to be about one so subject to
trembles   shows green in garment   is there
a Mrs Shoptaugh?   rustle up and snuggle
brilliant corners these are and have been all
the deal is raw crystals in a minister's dump truck
honey don't in bunches get delivered from
the skin's turning awful tight no more please
then he performed a shunt in daylight even
look Junior your idle hours also run on a schedule
saleable as gastropods sealed in lightning

SEÑOR BRANDS

A fourteenth century Italian silk damn-it
go get it man   don't let it strike
that's Bartell again clicking on a slove
he stains books and wakes up guilt-free
but I do not   I've never met
this the blood of an exact moment
District Attorney Arnold Murder speaks
all the hiss you'll ever need Mousketeer
try a hairnet or something even cooler
you dueler   I've studied your melt charts
they're all over the walls floated into portions
no redder a real nausea curing with touch
for God's sake Brando let's leaf through evil
get the bull figures   rife with a goat's occlusions

YOU CAN'T HAVE A PARTIAL LEMURIA

Don't go all horse spooky in the hockey nook
lessers have burned barns twisted props
gone all shank and clustered broom
a state of march and crustal cherryblock
a rosenblick tumbled then tempered
Somnambulistic Chuck he's regusted
Pacino's a perfect devil the rig he enjoys
unbarred   it's terrible an end to all vestment
barricade stunts in fog   you have a pencil?
sounds like family sprinkled and then heated
just so all the slightly furry locks clasp
oh dear there's a rhythm to that oh dear
depends on the you and not just any old dear
dry map of the moonlight on an oxygen blight

SHOP TALK
TALCUM TOP

Some tough phonecalls in an iron bucket
I had   the building nipped under me
they call it Mirrorville and it's on like toast
Doc or Fenway in Penury   a will that's awry
lemon sealant and everything like one big tense
sit down then and develop some traits dense?
yup   a defiance among the dark-eyed
don't care if you feel like it don't lock it
just see if you can knock it given   something
you're standing there you look down there's the float
you've been practicing those opportunities
jazzbos know   a dealbreaker's holiday
slunk down in wrap-up   a glisten log
how does it feel to lock the fog?

ANOTHER SAUCE

I hurt my hip on such a braided touch
just the thought of torpedoes those wet ends
cough in the soup   toss in the soap   I'll win
even blind with the crazies it's all temporal
the ovarian sailors will keep you up nights
unfold the tarry bracelets and ponder
no more loopy favors or indoor farms
it's all a matter of placement   three sprigs
salt the lens   the snow flakes   tiny poppers
draw the ears of a newt   kick the can
I'm off-center but nobody owns space
are you a bender or a spender it's crucial
the cylinder is no longer a pencil
the vacuum as crisp as your gorge

EPOCH AND SODA

It was like beating on a blood pie   stopping
off for a gel cap rung 'round with ex-custard
applied just barely to the lip the rosebud top
later suffering from nailover   on the mend?
not quite yet   so far so tight that
the window jumped   the car barn snapped
pumpkins come with their own extinguishers
the hardness of a haberdashery complex
controlled experiment or else convulsions
let me at that piano a Pinkerton I believe
as Miles smiles reverses all his numbers
backing the vehicle into itself it manages
Ashley Montague in a lemon disposition
and don't spare the Unguentine   pass the carbons

THE WAY CLEAR

Now we're in superspace even the tiniest
rivet is sentient   participating
particle emptiness proximal set
it's got to be around here someplace and closing
can't live long in a can   space is
a continual enhancement of the nonoriginary
hello Mother   don't knock it
there are spiral pitfalls   a collapse below
the infinitesimal though limitless leeway
your thought does not persist on most levels
transfers not   much of anywhere
points you can hear the valences lifting
gear-pure but cancel even that
go back you forgot the cat

GIVEN THE BOAT

My name's California   I snap to attention
there's this yellow block in my youth
I mark time by it   like going to the library
different font   no wife no looseness at all
we were wholly cherry   I refuse to apologize
anything at all that forms around my ammo
well how <u>does</u> one vote?   the embarcation point
please   some think I'm too   something
others think California is a steaming yellow pile
but I broke out   there was a nuclear impression
high as all Hades   you see the blades turning
there are always gross implications   diversions
we walk along a trench   you make mince
meat of my hat   insoluble at best

OP CIT LINGUAL OTHERS

Have a beep on me
he's reaching for the smoke
I came down with that once
Cape Bridger when the lamps failed
took out anything stationary
made a scene   not just partially
have a heart   what once
was fairly solid not quite encompassed
an arsenal of jellies here still
take yourself to mean anything?
broken exponents of strained primes
hold your bees dry   I'll handle the ladders
you perch or fly away Robin Blank
until the very point of this can't

RIGHT FOR ALL OCCASIONS
LEFT FOR NONE

I heard the shuttering stories
far above and way below us
a matter of rustless perimeters
science gets blamed again
hear those stuttering salmon?
precisely marked by radio
a blundering itchy storm so far
still wandering the old power plants
hike up your rubber pants for
this kitchen is filling with semen
even the parrots have flown
just imagine then hop on
an explosion made for that?
let's break out the happy maps

A SALVAGE

Cornerstone of all further stoppages
sits in the chamber with the victrola and stains her nails
goombye!   Penny Singleton would be a better choice
dangling crystal balls   armatures gone begging
jam jars later   take a look at this wonderful world
Saint Lesson here will trim off the bulk
there's not that much to speak of   curtsy at
the Dorseyland Band in a movie about Walking
in Portland the eastern one with the pond lights
the argon laps imagining scrimshaw melody
you expose your flesh to the drawn needles
the sun will always soak you   it's a battle for
the little clay dredger beached in your backyard
streams of one language through the clutter

 has a mission to redefine the terms of accessibility by publishing challenging writing distinguished by idiosyncrasy and intelligence rather than by allegiance with camps, schools, or cliques. It is part of our press's mission to support writers who might otherwise have difficulty being recognized because their work doesn't answer to either the mainstream or to recognizable modes of experimentation.

The Motherwell Prize is an annual series that offers publication of a first or second book of poems by a woman, as well as a one thousand dollar cash prize.

The Fence Modern Poets Series is open to poets of any gender and at any stage of career, and offers a one thousand dollar cash prize in addition to book publication.

For more information about either prize, or more informatin about Fence, visit www.fenceportal.org.

The Motherwell Prize

Negro League Baseball	Harmony Holiday
living must bury	Josie Sigler
Aim Straight at the Fountain and Press Vaporize	Elizabeth Marie Young
Unspoiled Air	Kaisa Ullsvik Miller

The Alberta Prize

The Cow	Ariana Reines
Practice, Restraint	Laura Sims
A Magic Book	Sasha Steensen
Sky Girl	Rosemary Griggs
The Real Moon of Poetry and Other Poems	Tina Brown Celona
Zirconia	Chelsey Minnis

Fence Modern Poets Series

The Other Poems	Paul Legault
Nick Demske	Nick Demske
Duties of an English Foreign Secretary	Macgregor Card
Star in the Eye	James Shea
Structure of the Embryonic Rat Brain	Christopher Janke
The Stupefying Flashbulbs	Daniel Brenner
Povel	Geraldine Kim
The Opening Question	Prageeta Sharma
Apprehend	Elizabeth Robinson
The Red Bird	Joyelle McSweeney

National Poetry Series

A Map Predetermined and Chance	Laura Wetherington
The Network	Jena Osman
The Black Automaton	Douglas Kearney
Collapsible Poetics Theater	Rodrigo Toscano

Anthologies & Critical Works

Not for Mothers Only: Contemporary Poets on Child-Getting & Child-Rearing
Catherine Wagner & Rebecca Wolff, editors

A Best of Fence: The First Nine Years, Volumes 1 & 2
Rebecca Wolff and Fence Editors, editors

Poetry

A Book Beginning What and Ending Away	Clark Coolidge
Mellow Actions	Brandon Downing
Mercury	Ariana Reines
Cœur de Lion	Ariana Reines
June	Daniel Brenner
English Fragments / A Brief History of the Soul	Martin Corless-Smith
The Sore Throat & Other Poems	Aaron Kunin
Dead Ahead	Ben Doller
Lake Antiquity	Brandon Downing
My New Job	Catherine Wagner
Stranger	Laura Sims
The Method	Sasha Steensen
The Orphan & Its Relations	Elizabeth Robinson
Site Acquisition	Brian Young
Rogue Hemlocks	Carl Martin
19 Names for Our Band	Jibade-Khalil Huffman
Infamous Landscapes	Prageeta Sharma
Bad Bad	Chelsey Minnis
Snip Snip!	Tina Brown Celona
Yes, Master	Michael Earl Craig
Swallows	Martin Corless-Smith
Folding Ruler Star	Aaron Kunin
The Commandrine & Other Poems	Joyelle McSweeney
Macular Hole	Catherine Wagner
Nota	Martin Corless-Smith
Father of Noise	Anthony McCann
Can You Relax in My House	Michael Earl Craig
Miss America	Catherine Wagner

Fiction

Prayer and Parable: Stories	Paul Maliszewski
Flet: A Novel	Joyelle McSweeney
The Mandarin	Aaron Kunin